Lover's Gift

and

RABINDRANATH TAGORE

Lover's Gift
and
Crossing

M

First edition 1918
Reprinted 1921, 1923, 1927, 1930, 1942, 1943, 1944
1945, 1947, 1949, 1954, 1960, 1961, 1965, 1968

MACMILLAN POCKET TAGORE EDITION
1980
Reprinted 1979, 1980, 1985

MACMILLAN INDIA LIMITED
Madras   Bombay   Delhi   Patna
Bangalore Hyderabad Lucknow Trivandrum
Associated companies throughout the world

SBN   033390 010 3

Published by S G Wasani for
Macmillan India Limited and printed by
T K Sengupta at Macmillan India Press, Madras 600 041

Lover's Gift

I

You allowed your kingly power to vanish, Shah Jahan, but your wish was to make imperishable a tear-drop of love.

Time has no pity for the human heart, he laughs at its sad struggle to remember.

You allured him with beauty, made him captive, and crowned the formless death with fadeless form.

The secret whispered in the hush of night to the ear of your love is wrought in the perpetual silence of stone.

Though empires crumble to dust, and centuries are lost in shadows, the marble still sighs to the stars, ' I remember. '

' I remember. '—But life forgets, for she has her call to the Endless: and she goes on her voyage unburdened, leaving her memories to the forlorn forms of beauty.

II

COME to my garden walk, my love. Pass by the fervid flowers that press themselves on your sight. Pass them by, stopping at some chance joy, which like a sudden wonder of sunset illumines, yet eludes.

For love's gift is shy, it never tells its name, it flits across the shade, spreading a shiver of joy along the dust. Overtake it or miss it for ever. But a gift that can be grasped is merely a frail flower, or a lamp with a flame that will flicker.

III

THE fruits come in crowds into my orchard, they jostle each other. They surge up in the light in an anguish of fullness.

Proudly step into my orchard, my queen, sit there in the shade, pluck the ripe fruits from their stems, and let them yield, to the utmost, their burden of sweetness at your lips.

In my orchard the butterflies shake their wings in the sun, the leaves tremble, the fruits clamour to come to completion.

IV

She is near to my heart as the meadow-flower to the earth; she is sweet to me as sleep is to tired limbs. My love for her is my life flowing in its fullness, like a river in autumn flood, running with serene abandonment. My songs are one with my love, like the murmur of a stream, that sings with all its waves and currents.

V

I would ask for still more, if I had the sky with all its stars, and the world with its endless riches; but I would be content with the smallest corner of this earth if only she were mine.

VI

In the light of this thriftless day of spring, my poet, sing of those who pass by and do not linger, who laugh as they run and never look back, who blossom in an hour of unreasoning delight, and fade in a moment without regret.

Do not sit down silently, to tell the beads of your past tears and smiles—do not stop to pick up the dropped petals from the flowers of overnight, do not go to seek things that evade you, to know the meaning that is not plain—leave the gaps in your life where they are, for the music to come out of their depths.

VII

IT is little that remains now, the rest was spent in one careless summer. It is just enough to put in a song and sing to you; to weave in a flower-chain gently clasping your wrist; to hang in your ear like a round pink pearl, like a blushing whisper; to risk in a game one evening and utterly lose.

My boat is a frail small thing, not fit for crossing wild waves in the rain. If you but lightly step on it I shall gently row you by the shelter of the shore, where the dark water in ripples is like a dream-ruffled sleep; where the dove's cooing from the drooping branches makes the noon-day shadows plaintive. At the day's end, when you are tired, I shall pluck a

dripping lily to put in your hair and take
my leave.

VIII

THERE is room for you. You are alone with
your few sheaves of rice. My boat is
crowded, it is heavily laden, but how can
I turn you away? your young body is slim
and swaying; there is a twinkling smile
in the edge of your eyes, and your robe is
coloured like the rain-cloud.

The travellers will land for different
roads and homes. You will sit for a while
on the prow of my boat, and at the jour-
ney's end none will keep you back.

Where do you go, and to what home,
to garner your sheaves? I will not ques-
tion you, but when I fold my sails and
moor my boat I shall sit and wonder in the
evening—Where do you go, and to what
home, to garner your sheaves?

IX

WOMAN, your basket is heavy, your limbs
are tired. For what distance have you set
out, with what hunger of profit? The way
is long, and the dust is hot in the sun.

See, the lake is deep and full, its water

7

dark like a crow's eye. The banks are sloping and tender with grass.

Dip your tired feet into the water. The noontide wind will pass its fingers through your hair; the pigeons will croon their sleep songs, the leaves will murmur the secrets that nestle in the shadows.

What matters it if the hours pass and the sun sets; if the way through the desolate land be lost in the waning light?

Yonder is my house, by the hedge of flowering *henna*; I will guide you. I will make a bed for you, and light a lamp. In the morning, when the birds are roused by the stir of milking the cows, I will waken you.

X

WHAT is it that drives these bees from their home; these followers of unseen trails? What cry is this in their eager wings? How can they hear the music that sleeps in the flower soul? How can they find their way to the chamber where the honey lies shy and silent?

XI

IT was only the budding of leaves in the

summer, the summer that came into the garden by the sea. It was only a stir and rustle in the south wind, a few lazy snatches of songs, and then the day was done.

But let there be flowering of love in the summer to come in the garden by the sea. Let my joy take its birth and clap its hands and dance with the surging songs, and make the morning open its eyes wide in sweet amazement.

XII

AGES ago when you opened the south gate of the garden of gods, and came down upon the first youth of the earth, O Spring; men and women rushed out of their houses, laughing and dancing, and pelting each other with flower-dust in a sudden madness of mirth.

Year after year you bring the same flowers that you scattered in your path in that earliest April. Therefore, today, in their pervading perfume, they breathe the sigh of the days that are now dreams—the clinging sadness of vanished worlds. Your breeze is laden with love-legends that have faded from all human language.

One day, with fresh wonder, you came into my life that was fluttered with its first love. Since then the tender timidness of that inexperienced joy comes hidden every year in the early green buds of your lemon flowers; your red roses carry in their burning silence all that was unutterable in me; the memory of lyric hours, those days of May, rustles in the thrill of your new leaves born again and again.

XIII

LAST night in the garden I offered you my youth's foaming wine. You lifted the cup to your lips, you shut your eyes and smiled while I raised your veil, unbound your tresses, drawing down upon my breast your face sweet with its silence, last night when the moon's dream overflowed the world of slumber.

Today in the dew-cooled calm of the dawn you are walking to God's temple, bathed and robed in white, with a basketful of flowers in your hand. I stand aside in the shade under the tree, with my head bent, in the calm of the dawn by the lonely road to the temple.

IF I am impatient today, forgive me, my
love. It is the first summer rain, and the
riverside forest is aflutter, and the blossom-
ing *kadam* trees are tempting the passing
winds with wine-cups of perfume. See,
from all corners of the sky lightnings are
darting their glances, and winds are
rampant in your hair.

If today I bring my homage to you,
forgive me, my love. The everyday world
is hidden in the dimness of the rain, all
work has stopped in the village, the mea-
dows are desolate. In your dark eyes the
coming of the rain finds its music, and it
is at your door that July waits with jas-
mines for your hair in its blue skirt.

XV

HER neighbours call her dark in the village
—but she is a lily to my heart, yes, a lily
though not fair. Light came muffled with
clouds when first I saw her in the field;
her head was bare, her veil was off, her
braided hair hanging loose on her neck.
She may be dark as they say in the village,
but I have seen her black eyes and am
glad.

The pulse of the air boded storm. She rushed out of the hut when she heard her dappled cow low in dismay. For a moment she turned her large eyes to the clouds, and felt a stir of the coming rain in the sky. I stood at the corner of the rice-field—if she noticed me, it was known only to her (and perhaps I know it). She is dark as the message of the shower in summer, dark as the shade of the flowering woodland; she is dark as the longing for unknown love in the wistful night of May.

XVI

SHE dwelt here by the pool with its landing-stairs in ruins. Many an evening she had watched the moon made dizzy by the shaking of bamboo leaves, and on many a rainy day the smell of the wet earth had come to her over the young shoots of rice.

Her pet name is known here among those date-palm groves and in the courtyards where girls sit and talk while stitching their winter quilts. The water in this pool keeps in its depth the memory of her swimming limbs, and her wet feet had left their marks, day after day, on the foot-path leading to the village.

12

The women who come today with their vessels to the water have all seen her smile over simple jests, and the old peasant, taking his bullocks to their bath, used to stop at her door everyday to greet her.

Many a sailing boat passes by this village; many a traveller takes rest beneath that banyan tree; the ferry boat crosses to yonder ford carrying crowds to the market; but they never notice this spot by the village road, near the pool with its ruined landing-stairs—where dwelt she whom I love.

XVII

WHILE ages passed and the bees haunted the summer gardens, the moon smiled to the lilies of the night, the lightnings flashed their fiery kisses to the clouds and fled laughing, the poet stood in a corner, one with the trees and clouds. He kept his heart silent, like a flower, watched through his dreams as does the crescent moon; and wandered like the summer breeze for no purpose.

One April evening, when the moon rose up like a bubble from the depth of the sunset; and one maiden was busy watering the plants; and one feeding her doe, and one making her peacock dance, the poet broke out singing—'Oh listen to the secrets of the world. I know that the lily is pale for the moon's love. The lotus draws her veil aside before the morning sun, and the reason is simple if you think. The meaning of the bee's hum in the ear of the early jasmine has escaped the learned, but the poet knows. '

The sun went down in a blaze of blush, the moon loitered behind the trees, and the south wind whispered to the lotus that the poet was not as simple as he seemed. The maidens and youths clapped their hands and cried—' The world's secret is out. ' They looked into each other's eye and sang—' Let our secret as well be flung into the winds. '

XVIII

YOUR days will be full of cares, if you must give me your heart. My house by the cross-roads has its doors open and my mind is absent—for I sing.

I shall never be made to answer for it, if you must give me your heart. If I pledge my word to you in tunes now, and am too much in earnest to keep it when music is silent, you must forgive me; for the law laid down in May is best broken in December.

Do not always keep remembering it, if you must give me your heart. When your eyes sing with love, and your voice ripples with laughter, my answers to your questions will be wild, and not miserly accurate in facts—they are to be believed for ever and then forgotten for good.

XIX

IT is written in the book that Man, when fifty, must leave the noisy world, to go to the forest seclusion. But the poet proclaims that the forest hermitage is only for the young. For it is the birthplace of flowers and the haunt of birds and bees; and hidden nooks are waiting there for the thrill of lovers' whispers. There the moonlight, that is all one kiss for the *mālatī* flowers, has its deep message, but those who understand it are far below fifty.

And alas, youth is inexperienced and wilful, therefore it is but meet that the old should take charge of the household, and the young take to the seclusion of forest shades and the severe discipline of courting.

WHERE is the market for you, my song? Is it there where the learned muddle the summer breeze with their snuff; where men endlessly dispute whether the oil depends upon the cask, or the cask upon the oil; where yellow manuscripts frown upon the fleet footed frivolousness of life? My song cries out, Ah, no, no, no.

. Where is the market for you, my song? Is it there where the man of fortune grows enormous in pride and flesh in his marble palace, with his books on the shelves, dressed in leather, painted in gold, dusted by slaves, their virgin pages dedicated to the god obscure? My song gasped and said, Ah, no, no, no.

Where is the market for you, my song? Is it there where the young student sits, with his head bent over his books, and his mind straying in youth's dream-land; where prose is prowling on the desk, and poetry hiding in the heart? There among that dusty disorder, would you care to play hide-and-seek? My song remains silent in shy hesitation.

Where is the market for you, my song? Is it there where the bride is busy in the house, where she runs to her bedroom the moment she is free, and snatches, from under her pillows, the book of romance so roughly handled by the baby, so full of the scent of her hair? My song heaves a sigh and trembles with uncertain desire.

Where is the market for you, my song? Is it there where the least of a bird's notes is never missed, where the stream's babbling finds its full wisdom, where all the lute-strings of the world shower their music upon two fluttering hearts? My song bursts out and cries, Yes, yes.

XXI

(From the Bengali of DEVENDRANATH SEN)

METHINKS, my love, before the daybreak of life you stood under some waterfall of happy dreams, filling your blood with its liquid turbulence. Or, perhaps, your path was through the garden of the gods, where the merry multitude of jasmine, lilies, and oleanders fell into your arms in heaps, and entering your heart became boister-ous.

Your laughter is a song whose words are drowned in the clamour of tunes, a rapture of the odour of flowers unseen; it is like the moonlight breaking through the window of your lips when the moon is hiding in your heart. I ask for no reason, I forget the cause, I only know that your laughter is the tumult of insurgent life.

XXII

I SHALL gladly suffer the pride of culture to die out in my house, if only in some happy future I am born a herd boy in the Brinda forest.

The herd boy who grazes his cattle sitting under the banyan tree, and idly weaves *gunja* flowers into garlands, who loves to splash and plunge in the Jamuna's cool deep stream.

He calls his companions to wake up when morning dawns, and all the houses in the lane hum with the sound of the churn, clouds of dust are raised by the cattle, the maidens come out in the courtyard to milk the kine.

As the shadows deepen under the *tomal* trees, and the dusk gathers on the riverbanks; when the milkmaids, while crossing the turbulent water, tremble with fear; and loud peacocks, with tails outspread, dance in the forest, he watches the summer clouds.

When the April night is sweet as a fresh-blown flower, he disappears in the forest with a peacock's plume in his hair; the swing ropes are twined with flowers on the branches; the south wind throbs with music, and the merry shepherd boys crowd on the banks of the blue river.

No, I will never be the leader, brothers, of this new age of new Bengal; I shall not trouble to light the lamp of culture for the benighted. If only I could be born, under the shady *ashoka* groves, in some village of Brinda, where milk is churned by the maidens.

XXIII

I LOVED the sandy bank where, in the lonely pools, ducks clamoured and turtles basked in the sun; where, with evening, stray fishing-boats took shelter in the shadow by the tall grass.

You loved the wooded bank where shadows were gathered in the arms of the bamboo thickets; where women came with their vessels through the winding lane.

The same river flowed between us, singing the same song to both its banks. I listened to it, lying alone on the sand under the stars; and you listened sitting by the edge of the slope in the early morning light. Only the words I heard from it you did not know, and the secret it spoke to you was a mystery forever to me.

XXIV

YOUR window half-opened and veil half-raised you stand there waiting for the bangle-seller to come with his tinsel. You idly watch the heavy cart creak on in the dusty road, and the boat-mast crawling along the horizon across the far-off river.

The world to you is like an old woman's chant at her spinning-wheel, unmeaning rhymes crowded with random images.

But who knows if he is on his way this lazy sultry noon, the Stranger, carrying his basket of strange wares? He will pass by your door with his clear cry, and you shall fling open your window, cast off your veil, come out of the dusk of your dreams and meet your destiny.

XXV

I CLASP your hands, and my heart plunges into the dark of your eyes, seeking you, who ever evade me behind words and silence.

Yet I know that I must be content

in my love, with what is fitful and fugitive.
For we have met for a moment in the
crossing of the roads. Have I the power to
carry you through this crowd of worlds,
through this maze of paths? Have I the
food that can sustain you across the dark
passage gaping with arches of death?

XXVI

IF by chance you think of me, I shall sing
to you when the rainy evening loosens her
shadows upon the river, slowly trailing
her dim light towards the west—when
the day's remnant is too narrow for work
or for play.

You will sit alone in the balcony of the
south, and I shall sing from the darkened
room.   In the growing dusk the smell of
the wet leaves will come through the win-
dow; and the stormy winds will become
clamorous in the coconut grove.

When the lighted lamp is brought into
the room I shall go. And then, perhaps,
you will listen to the night, and hear my
song when I am silent.

XXVII

I FILLED my tray with whatever I had,

and gave it to you. What shall I bring to your feet tomorrow, I wonder? I am like the tree that, at the end of the flowering summer, gazes at the sky with its lifted branches bare of their blossoms.

But in all my past offerings is there not a single flower made fadeless by the eternity of tears?

Will you remember it and thank me with your eyes when I stand before you with empty hands at the leave-taking of my summer days?

XXVIII

I DREAMT that she sat by my head, tenderly ruffling my hair with her fingers, playing the melody of her touch. I looked at her face and struggled with my tears, till the agony of unspoken words burst my sleep like a bubble.

I sat up and saw the glow of the Milky Way above my window, like a world of silence on fire, and I wondered if at this moment she had a dream that rhymed with mine.

XXIX

I THOUGHT I had something to say to her

when our eyes met across the hedge. But
she passed away. And it rocks day and
night, like a boat, on every wave of the
hours, the word that I had to say to her.
It seems to sail in the autumn clouds on an
endless quest and to bloom into evening
flowers, seeking its lost moment in the
sunset. It twinkles like fireflies in my heart,
to find its meaning in the dusk of despair,
the word that I had to say to Her.

XXX

THE spring flowers break out like the pas-
sionate pain of unspoken love.   With their
breath comes the memory of my old day
songs.   My heart of a sudden has put on
green leaves of desire.   My love came not,
but her touch is in my limbs, and her
voice comes across the fragrant fields. Her
gaze is in the sad depth of the sky, but
where are her eyes? Her kisses flit in the
air, but where are her lips?

XXXI

A POSY

(From the Bengali of SATYENDRANATH DATTA)
MY flowers were like milk and honey and

wine; I bound them into a posy with a golden ribbon, but they escaped my watchful care and fled away, and only the ribbon remains.

My songs were like milk and honey and wine, they were held in the rhythm of my beating heart, but they spread their wings and fled away, the darlings of the idle hours, and my heart beats in silence.

The beauty I loved was like milk and honey and wine, her lips like the rose of the dawn, her eyes bee-black. I kept my heart silent lest it should startle her, but she eluded me like my flowers and like my songs, and my love remains alone.

XXXII

MANY a time when the spring day knocked at our door I kept busy with my work and you did not answer. Now when I am left alone and heartsick the spring day comes once again, but I know not how to turn him away from the door. When he came to crown us with joy the gate was shut, but now when he comes with his gift of sorrow his path must be open.

XXXIII

THE boisterous spring, who once came into my life with its lavish laughter, burdening her hours with improvident roses, setting skies aflame with the red kisses of new-born *ashoka* leaves, now comes stealing into my solitude through the lonely lanes along the brooding shadows heavy with silence, and sits still in my balcony gazing across the fields, where the green of the earth swoons exhausted in the utter paleness of the sky.

XXXIV

WHEN our farewell moment came, like a low-hanging rain-cloud, I had only time to tie a red ribbon on your wrist, while my hands trembled. Today I sit alone on the grass in the season of *mahua* flowers, with one quivering question in my mind, ' Do you still keep the little red ribbon tied on your wrist ? '

You went by the narrow road that skirted the blossoming field of flax. I saw that my garland of overnight was still hanging loose from your hair. But why did you not wait till I could gather, in the morning, new flowers for my final gift?

I wonder if unawares it dropped on your way—the garland hanging loose from your hair.

Many a song I had sung to you, morning and evening, and the last one you carried in your voice when you went away. You never tarried to hear the one song unsung I had for you alone and forever. I wonder if, at last, you are tired of my song that you hummed to yourself while walking through the field.

XXXV

LAST night clouds were threatening, and *amlak* branches struggled in the grips of the gusty wind. I hoped, if dreams came to me, they would come in the shape of my beloved, in the lonely night loud with rain.

The winds still moan through the fields, and the tear-stained cheeks of dawn are pale. My dreams have been in vain, for truth is hard, and dreams, too, have their own ways.

Last night when the darkness was drunken with storm, and the rain, like night's veil, was torn by the winds into shreds, would it make truth jealous if untruth came to me in the shape of my beloved, in the starless night loud with rain?

XXXVI

My fetters, you made music in my heart. I played with you all day long and made you my ornament. We were the best of friends, my fetters. There were times when I was afraid of you, but my fear made me love you the more. You were companions of my long dark night, and I make my bow to you, before I bid you good-bye, my fetters.

XXXVII

You had your rudder broken many a time, my boat, and your sails torn to tatters. Often had you drifted towards the sea, dragging anchor, and heeded not. But now there has spread a crack in your hull and your hold is heavy. Now is the time for you to end your voyage, to be rocked into sleep by lapping of the water by the beach.

Alas, I know all warning is vain. The veiled face of dark doom lures you. The madness of the storm and the waves is upon you. The music of the tide is rising high.   You are shaken by the fever of that dance.

Then break your chain, my boat, and be free, and fearlessly rush to your wreck.

XXXVIII

THE current in which I drifted ran rapid and strong when I was young. The spring breeze was spendthrift of itself, the trees were on fire with flowers; and the birds never slept from singing.

I sailed with giddy speed, carried away by the flood of passion; I had no time to see and feel and take the world into my being.

Now that youth has ebbed and I am stranded on the bank, I can hear the deep music of all things, and the sky opens to me its heart of stars.

XXXIX

THERE is a looker-on who sits behind my eyes.   It seems he has seen things in ages and worlds beyond memory's shore, and those forgotten sights glisten on the grass and shiver on the leaves. He has seen under new veils the face of the one beloved, in twilight hours of many a nameless star.

Therefore his sky seems to ache with the pain of countless meetings and partings, and a longing pervades this spring breeze, —the longing that is full of the whisper of ages without beginning.

XL

A MESSAGE came from my youth of vanished days, saying, ' I wait for you among the quiverings of unborn May, where smiles ripen for tears and hours ache with songs unsung.'

It says, ' Come to me across the worn-out track of age, through the gates of death. For dreams fade, hopes fail, the gathered fruits of the year decay, but I am the eternal truth, and you shall meet me again and again in your voyage of life from shore to shore.'

XLI

THE girls are out to fetch water from the river—their laughter comes through the trees, I long to join them in the lane, where goats graze in the shade, and squirrels flit from sun to shadow, across the fallen leaves.

But my day's task is already done, my

jars are filled. I stand at my door to watch the glistening green of the *areca* leaves, and hear the laughing women going to fetch water from the river.

It has ever been dear to me to carry the burden of my full vessel day after day, in the dew-dipped morning freshness and in the tired glimmer of the dayfall.

Its gurgling water babbled to me when my mind was idle, it laughed with the silent laughter of my joyous thoughts—it spoke to my heart with tearful sobs when I was sad. I have carried it in stormy days, when the loud rain drowned the anxious cooing of doves.

My day's task is done, my jars are filled, the light wanes in the west, and shadows gather beneath the trees; a sigh comes from the flowering linseed field, and my wistful eyes follow the lane that runs through the village to the bank of the dark water.

XLII

ARE you a mere picture, and not as true as those stars, true as this dust? They throb with the pulse of things, but you are immensely aloof in your stillness, painted form.

The day was when you walked with me, your breath warm, your limbs singing of life. My world found its speech in your voice, and touched my heart with your face. You suddenly stopped in your walk, in the shadow-side of the Forever, and I went on alone.

Life, like a child, laughs, shaking its rattle of death as it runs; it beckons me on, I follow the unseen; but you stand there, where you stopped behind that dust and those stars; and you are a mere picture.

No, it cannot be. Had the life flood utterly stopped in you, it would stop the river in its flow, and the foot-fall of dawn in her cadence of colours. Had the glimmering dusk of your hair vanished in the hopeless dark, the woodland shade of summer would die with its dreams.

Can it be true that I forgot you? We haste on without heed, forgetting the flowers on the roadside hedge. Yet they breathe unaware into our forgetfulness, filling it with music. You have moved from my world, to take seat at the root of my life, and therefore is this forgetting —remembrance lost in its own depth.

You are no longer before my songs, but one with them. You came to me with the

first ray of dawn. I lost you with the last
gold of evening. Ever since I am always
finding you through the dark. No, you
are no mere picture.

XLIII

DYING, you have left behind you the great
sadness of the Eternal in my life. You
have painted my thought's horizon with
the sunset colours of your departure, leav-
ing a track of tears across the earth to love's
heaven. Clasped in your dear arms, life and
death united in me in a marriage bond.

I think I can see you watching there in
the balcony with your lamp lighted, where
the end and the beginning of all things
meet. My world went hence through the
doors that you opened—you holding the
cup of death to my lips, filling it with life
from your own.

XLIV

WHEN in your death you died to all that
was outside me, vanishing from the thou-
sand things of the world, to be fully reborn
in my sorrow, I felt that my life had grown
perfect, the man and the woman becoming
one in me forever.

BRING beauty and order into my forlorn
life, woman, as you brought them into
my house when you lived. Sweep away
the dusty fragments of the hours, fill the
empty jars and mend all neglects. Then
open the inner door of the shrine, light
the candle, and let us meet there in silence
before our God.

XLVI

THE sky gazes on its own endless blue and
dreams. We clouds are its whims, we have
no home. The stars shine on the crown of
Eternity. Their records are permanent,
while ours are pencilled, to be rubbed off
the next moment. Our part is to appear on
the stage of the air to sound our tam-
bourines and fling flashes of laughter.
But from our laughter comes the rain,
which is real enough, and thunder which
is no jest. Yet we have no claim upon Time
for wages, and the breath that blew us into
being blows us away before we are given
a name.

XLVII

THE road is my wedded companion. She

speaks to me under my feet all day, she sings to my dreams all night.

My meeting with her had no beginning, it begins endlessly at each daybreak, renewing its summer in fresh flowers and songs, and her every new kiss is the first kiss to me.

The road and I are lovers. I change my dress for her night after night, leaving the tattered cumber of the old in the wayside inns when the day dawns.

XLVIII

I TRAVELLED the old road everyday, I took my fruits to the market, my cattle to the meadows, I ferried my boat across the stream and all the ways were well known to me.

One morning my basket was heavy with wares. Men were busy in the fields, the pastures crowded with cattle; the breast of earth heaved with the mirth of ripening rice.

Suddenly there was a tremor in the air, and the sky seemed to kiss me on my forehead. My mind started up like the morning out of mist.

I forgot to follow the track. I stepped a few paces from the path, and my familiar world appeared strange to me, like a flower I had only known in bud.

My everyday wisdom was ashamed. I went astray in the fairyland of things. It was the best luck of my life that I lost my path that morning, and found my eternal childhood.

XLIX

WHERE is heaven? you ask me, my child, —the sages tell us it is beyond the limits of birth and death, unswayed by the rhythm of day and night; it is not of this earth.

But your poet knows that its eternal hunger is for time and space, and it strives evermore to be born in the fruitful dust. Heaven is fulfilled in your sweet body, my child, in your palpitating heart.

The sea is beating its drums in joy, the flowers are a tip-toe to kiss you. For heaven is born in you, in the arms of the mother-dust.

THE CHILD

(Translated from the Bengali of
Dwÿendralál Roy)

' Come, moon, come down, kiss my darling on the forehead,' cries the mother as she holds the baby girl in her lap while the moon smiles as it dreams. There come stealing in the dark the vague fragrance of the summer and the night-bird's songs from the shadow-laden solitude of the mango-grove. At a far-away village rises from a peasant's flute a fountain of plaintive notes, and the young mother, sitting on the terrace, baby in her lap, croons sweetly, ' Come, moon, come down, kiss my darling on the forehead.' Once she looks up at the light of the sky, and then at the light of the earth in her arms, and I wonder at the placid silence of the moon.

The baby laughs and repeats her mother's call, ' Come, moon, come down.' The mother smiles, and smiles the moonlit night, and I, the poet, the husband of the baby's mother, watch this picture from behind, unseen.

THE early autumn day is cloudless. The river is full to the brim, washing the naked roots of the tottering tree by the ford. The long narrow path, like the thirsty tongue of the village, dips down into the stream.

My heart is full, as I look around me and see the silent sky and the flowing water, and feel that happiness is spread abroad, as simply as a smile on a child's face.

LII

TIRED of waiting, you burst your bonds, impatient flowers, before the winter had gone. Glimpses of the unseen comer reached your wayside watch, and you rushed out running and panting, impulsive jasmines, troops of riotous roses.

You were the first to march to the breach of death, your clamour of colour and perfume troubled the air. You laughed and pressed and pushed each other, bared your breast and dropped in heaps.

The Summer will come in its time, sailing in the flood-tide of the south wind. But you never counted slow moments to be sure of him. You recklessly spent your all in the road, in the terrible joy of faith.

You heard his footsteps from afar, and flung your mantle of death for him to tread upon. Your bonds break even before the rescuer is seen, you make him your own ere he can come and claim you.

LIII

CHAMPA

(From the Bengali of SATYENDRANATH DATTA)

I OPENED my bud when April breathed her last and the summer scorched with kisses the unwilling earth. I came half afraid and half curious, like a mischievous imp peeping at a hermit's cell.

I heard the frightened whispers of the despoiled woodland, and the *Kokil* gave voice to the languor of the summer; through the fluttering leaf-curtain of my birth-chamber I saw the world grim, grey, and haggard.

Yet boldly I came out strong with the faith of youth, quaffed the fiery wine from the glowing bowl of the sky, and proudly saluted the morning, I, the champa flower, who carry the perfume of the sun in my heart.

In the beginning of time, there rose from the churning of God's dream two women. One is the dancer at the court of paradise, the desired of men, she who laughs and plucks the minds of the wise from their cold meditations and of fools from their emptiness; and scatters them like seeds with careless hands in the extravagant winds of March, in the flowering frenzy of May.

The other is the crowned queen of heaven, the mother, throned on the fullness of golden autumn; she who in the harvest-time brings straying hearts to the smile sweet as tears, the beauty deep as the sea of silence—brings them to the temple of the Unknown, at the holy confluence of Life and Death.

LV

THE noonday air is quivering, like the gauzy wings of a dragon-fly. Roofs of the village huts brood birdlike over the drowsy households, while a *Kokil* sings unseen from its leafy loneliness.

The fresh liquid notes drop upon the tuneless toil of the human crowd, adding music to lovers' whispers, to mothers' kisses, to children's laughter. They flow over our thoughts, like a stream over pebbles, rounding them in beauty every unconscious moment.

LVI

THE evening was lonely for me, and I was reading a book till my heart became dry, and it seemed to me that beauty was a thing fashioned by the traders in words. Tired I shut the book and snuffed the candle. In a moment the room was flooded with moonlight.

Spirit of Beauty, how could you, whose radiance overbrims the sky, stand hidden behind a candle's tiny flame? How could a few vain words from a book rise like a mist, and veil her whose voice has hushed the heart of earth into ineffable calm?

LVII

THIS autumn is mine, for she was rocked in my heart. The glistening bells of her anklets rang in my blood, and her misty veil fluttered in my breath. I know the touch of her blown hair in all my dreams. She is abroad in the trembling leaves that

danced in my life-throbs, and her eyes
that smile from the blue sky drank their
light from me.

LVIII

THINGS throng and laugh loud in the sky;
the sands and dust dance and whirl like
children. Man's mind is aroused by their
shouts; his thoughts long to be the play-
mates of things.

Our dreams, drifting in the stream of
the vague, stretch their arms to clutch the
earth—their efforts stiffen into bricks and
stones, and thus the city of man is built.

Voices come swarming from the past—
seeking answers from the living moments.
Beats of their wings fill the air with tre-
mulous shadows, and sleepless thoughts in
our minds leave their nests to take flight
across the desert of dimness, in the pas-
sionate thirst for forms. They are lampless
pilgrims, seeking the shore of light, to find
themselves in things. They will be lured
into poet's rhymes, they will be housed in
the towers of the town not yet planned,
they have their call to arms from the
battlefields of the future, they are bidden
to join hands in the strifes of peace yet to
come.

THEY do not build high towers in the
Land of All-I-Have-Found. A grassy lawn
runs by the road, with a stream of fugitive
water at its side. The bees haunt the cot-
tage porches abloom with passion flowers.
The men set out on their errands with a
smile, and in the evening they come home
with a song, with no wages, in the Land
of All-I-Have-Found.

In the midday, sitting in the cool of
their courtyards, the women hum and
spin at their wheels, while over the waving
harvest comes wafted the music of shep-
herds' flutes. It rejoices the wayfarers'
hearts who walk singing through the shim-
mering shadows of the fragrant forest in
the Land of All-I-Have-Found.

The traders sail with their merchandise
down the river, but they do not moor their
boats in this land; soldiers march with
banners flying, but the king never stops
his chariot. Travellers who come from
afar to rest here awhile, go away without
knowing what there is in the Land of All-I-
Have-Found.

Here crowds do not jostle each other
in the roads. O poet, set up your house
in this land. Wash from your feet the dust

of distant wanderings, tune your lute, and at the day's end stretch yourself on the cool grass under the evening star in the Land of All-I-Have-Found.

LX

TAKE back your coins, King's Councillor. I am of those women you sent to the forest shrine to decoy the young ascetic who had never seen a woman. I failed in your bidding.

Dimly day was breaking when the hermit boy came to bathe in the stream, his tawny locks crowded on his shoulders, like a cluster of morning clouds, and his limbs shining like a streak of sunbeam. We laughed and sang as we rowed in our boat; we jumped into the river in a mad frolic, and danced around him, when the sun rose staring at us from the water's edge in a flush of divine anger.

Like a child-god, the boy opened his eyes and watched our movements, the wonder deepening till his eyes shone like morning stars. He lifted his clasped hands and chanted a hymn of praise in his bird-like young voice, thrilling every leaf of the forest. Never such words were sung to a mortal woman before; they were like the

43

silent hymn to the dawn which rises from the hushed hills. The women hid their mouths with their hands, their bodies swaying with laughter, and a spasm of doubt ran across his face. Quickly came I to his side, sorely pained, and, bowing to his feet, I said, 'Lord, accept my service.'

I led him to the grassy bank, wiped his body with the end of my silken mantle, and, kneeling on the ground, I dried his feet with my trailing hair. When I raised my face and looked into his eyes, I thought I felt the world's first kiss to the first woman—Blessed am I, blessed is God, who made me a woman. I heard him say to me, 'What God unknown are you? Your touch is the touch of the Immortal, your eyes have the mystery of the midnight.'

Ah, no, not that smile, King's Councillor—the dust of worldly wisdom has covered your sight, old man. But this boy's innocence pierced the mist and saw the shining truth, the woman divine.

Ah, how the goddess wakened in me, at the awful light of that first adoration. Tears filled my eyes, the morning ray caressed my hair like a sister, and the woodland breeze kissed my forehead as it kisses the flowers.

The women clapped their hands, and laughed their obscene laugh, and with veils dragging on the dust and hair hanging loose they began to pelt him with flowers.

Alas, my spotless sun, could not my shame weave fiery mist to cover you in its folds? I fell at his feet and cried, ' Forgive me.' I fled like a stricken deer through shade and sun, and cried as I fled, ' Forgive me. ' The women's foul laughter pressed me like a crackling fire, but the words ever rang in my ears, ' What God unknown are you? '

Crossing

I

THE sun breaks out from the clouds on the day when I must go.

And the sky gazes upon the earth like God's wonder.

My heart is sad, for it knows not from where comes its call.

Does the breeze bring the whisper of the world which I leave behind with its music of tears melting in the sunny silence? or the breath of the island in the far-away sea basking in the Summer of the unknown flowers?

II

WHEN the market is over and they return
   homewards through the dusk,.
I sit at the wayside to watch thee plying
   thy boat,
Crossing the dark water with the sunset
   gleam upon thy sail;
I see thy silent figure standing at the helm
   and suddenly catch thy eyes gazing
   upon me;
I leave my song; and cry to thee to take
   me across.

III

THE wind is up, I set my sail of songs,
Steersman, sit at the helm.
For my boat is fretting to be free, to dance
   in the rhythm of the wind and water.
The day is spent, it is evening.
My friends of the shore have taken leave.
Loose the chain and heave the anchor,
   we sail by the starlight.
The wind is stirred into the murmur of
   music at this time of my departure.
Steersman, sit at the helm.

IV

ACCEPT me, my lord, accept me for this while.

Let those orphaned days that passed without thee be forgotten.

Only spread this little moment wide across thy lap, holding it under thy light.

I have wandered in pursuit of voices that drew me yet led me nowhere.

Now let me sit in peace and listen to thy words in the soul of my silence.

Do not turn away thy face from my heart's dark secrets, but burn them till they are alight with thy fire.

V

THE scouts of a distant storm have pitched their cloud-tents in the sky; the light has paled; the air is damp with tears in the voiceless shadows of the forest.

The peace of sadness is in my heart like the brooding silence upon the master's lute before the music begins.

My world is still with the expectation of the great pain of thy coming into my life.

VI

Thou hast done well, my lover, thou hast done well to send me thy fire of pain.

For my incense never yields its perfume till it burns, and my lamp is blind till it is lighted.

When my mind is numb its torpor must be stricken by thy love's lightning; and the very darkness that blots my world burns like a torch when set afire by thy thunder.

VII

Deliver me from my own shadows, my lord, from the wrecks and confusion of my days.

For the night is dark and thy pilgrim is blinded,

Hold thou my hand.

Deliver me from despair.

Touch with thy flame the lightless lamp of my sorrow.

Waken my tired strength from its sleep.

Do not let me linger behind counting my losses.

Let the road sing to me of the house at every step.

For the night is dark, and thy pilgrim is
   blinded.
Hold thou my hand.

VIII

THE lantern which I carry in my hand
   makes enemy of the darkness of the
   farther road.
And this wayside becomes a terror to me,
   where even the flowering tree frowns
   like a spectre of scowling menace; and
   the sound of my own steps comes
   back to me in the echo of muffled
   suspicion.
Therefore I pray for thy own morning
   light, when the far and the near will
   kiss each other and death and life will
   be one in love.

IX

WHEN thou savest me the steps are lighter
   in the march of thy worlds.
When stains are washed away from my
   heart it brightens the light of thy sun.
That the bud has not blossomed in beauty
   in my life spreads sadness in the heart
   of creation.
When the shroud of darkness will be lifted

from my soul it will bring music to thy
smile.

X

THOU hast given me thy love, filling the
world with thy gifts.

They are showered upon me when I do
not know them, for my heart is asleep
and dark is the night.

Yet though lost in the cavern of my
dreams I have been thrilled with fitful
gladness;

And I know that in return for the treasure
of thy great worlds thou wilt receive
from me one little flower of love in the
morning when my heart awakes.

XI

MY eyes have lost their sleep in watching;
yet if I do not meet thee still it is sweet
to watch.

My heart sits in the shadow of the rains
waiting for thy love; if she is deprived
still it is sweet to hope.

They walk away in their different paths
leaving me behind; if I am alone still it
is sweet to listen for thy footsteps.

The wistful face of the earth weaving its

autumn mists wakens longing in my heart; if it is in vain still it is sweet to feel the pain of longing.

XII

HOLD thy faith firm, my heart, the day will dawn.

The seed of promise is deep in the soil, it will sprout.

Sleep, like a bud, will open its heart to the light, and the silence will find its voice.

The day is near when thy burden will become thy gift, and thy sufferings will light up thy path.

XIII

THE wedding hour is in the twilight, when the birds have sung their last and the winds are at rest on the waters, when the sunset spreads the carpet in the bridal chamber and the lamp is made ready to burn through the night.

Behind the silent dark walks the Unseen Comer and my heart trembles.

All songs are hushed, for the service will be read under the evening star.

XIV

In the night when noise is tired the murmur of the sea fills the air.

The vagrant desires of the day come back to their rest round the lighted lamp.

Love's play is stilled into worship, life's stream touches the deep, and the world of forms comes to its nest in the beauty beyond all forms.

XV

Who is awake all alone in this sleeping earth, in the air drowsing among the moveless leaves? awake in the silent birds' nests, in the secret centres of the flower buds? awake in the throbbing stars of the night, in the depth of the pain of my being?

XVI

You came to my door in the dawn and sang; it angered me to be awakened from sleep, and you went away unheeded.

You came in the noon and asked for water; it vexed me in my work, and you were sent away with reproaches.

You came in the evening with your flam-
  ing torches.
You seemed to me like a terror and I shut
  my door.
Now in the midnight I sit alone in my
  lampless room and call you back whom
  I turned away in insult.

XVII

PICK up this life of mine from the dust.
Keep it under your eyes, in the palm of
  your right hand.
Hold it up in the light, hide it under the
  shadow of death; keep it in the casket
  of the night with your stars, and then
  in the morning let it find itself among
  flowers that blossom in worship.

XVIII

I KNOW that this life, missing its ripeness
  in love, is not altogether lost.
I know that the flowers that fade in the
  dawn, the streams that strayed in the
  desert, are not altogether lost.
I know that whatever lags behind in this
  life laden with slowness is not altogether
  lost.
I know that my dreams that are still un-

fulfilled, and my melodies still unstruck,
are clinging to some lute-strings of
thine, and they are not altogether lost.

XIX

You came to me in the wayward hours of
spring with flute songs and flowers.
You troubled my heart from ripples into
waves, rocking the red lotus of love.
You asked me to come out with you into
the secret of life.
But I fell asleep among the murmurous
leaves of May.
When I woke the cloud gathered in the
sky and the dead leaves flitted in the
wind.
Through the patter of rain I hear your
nearing footsteps and the cry to come
out with you into the secret of
death.
I walk to your side and put my hand into
yours, while your eyes burn and water
drips from your hair.

XX

The day is dim with rain.
Angry lightnings glance through the tat-
tered cloud-veils.

And the forest is like a caged lion shaking
 its mane in despair.
On such a day amidst the winds beating
 their wings, let me find my peace in
 thy presence.
For the sorrowing sky has shadowed my
 solitude, to deepen the meaning of thy
 touch about my heart.

XXI

On that night when the storm broke open
 my door
I did not know that you entered my room
 through the ruins,
For the lamp was blown out, and it be-
 came dark;
I stretched my arms to the sky in search
 of help.
I lay on the dust waiting in the tumultuous
 dark and I knew not that storm was
 your own banner.
When the morning came I saw you stand-
 ing upon the emptiness that was spread
 over my house.

XXII

Is it the Destroyer who comes?

For the boisterous sea of tears heaves in
the flood-tide of pain.

The crimson clouds run wild in the wind
lashed by lightning, and the thunder-
ing laughter of the Mad is over the sky.

Life sits in the chariot crowned by Death.

Bring out your tribute to him of all that
you have.

Do not hug your savings to your heart, do
not look behind,

Bend your head at his feet, trailing your
hair in the dust.

Take to the road from this moment.

For the lamp is blown out and the house
is desolate.

The storm winds scream through your
doors, the walls are rocking, and the
call comes from the land of dimness
beyond your ken.

Hide not your face in terror; tears are in
vain; your door-chains have snapped.

Run out for your voyage to the end of all
joys and sorrows.

Let your steps be the steps of a desperate
dance.

Sing 'Victory to Life in Death.'

Accept your destiny, O Bride!

Put on your red robe to follow through
the darkness the torchlight of the Bride-
groom!

60

XXIII

I CAME nearest to you, though I did not
know it when I came to hurt you.

I owned you at last as my master when I
fought against you to be defeated.

I merely made my debt to you burden-
some when I robbed you in secret.

I struggled in my pride against your cur-
rent only to feel all your force in my
breast.

Rebelliously I put out the light in my
house and your sky surprised me with
its stars.

XXIV

HAVE you come to me as my sorrow? All
the more I must cling to you.

Your face is veiled in the dark, all the
more I must see you.

At the blow of death from your hand let
my life leap up in a flame.

Tears flow from my eyes—let them flow
round your feet in worship.

And let the pain in my breast speak to me
that you are still mine.

XXV

I HID myself to evade you.

Now that I am caught at last, strike me,
see if I flinch.

Finish the game for good.

If you win in the end, strip me of all that
I have.

I have had my laughter and songs in
wayside booths and stately halls—
now that you have come into my life,
make me weep, see if you can break
my heart.

XXVI

WHEN I awake in thy love my night of
ease will be ended.

Thy sunrise will touch my heart with its
touchstone of fire, and my voyage will
begin in its orbit of triumphant suffer-
ing.

I shall dare to take up death's challenge
and carry thy voice in the heart of
mockery and menace.

I shall bare my breast against the wrongs
hurled at thy children, and take the
risk of standing by thy side where none
but thee remains.

XXVII

I AM the weary earth of summer bare
    life and parched.
I wait for thy shower to come down in the
    night when I open my breast and receive
    it in silence.
I long to give thee in return my songs and
    flowers.
But empty is my store, and only the deep
    sigh rises from my heart through the
    withered grass.
But I know that thou wilt wait for the
    morning when my hours will brim with
    their riches.

XXVIII

COME to me like summer cloud, spreading
    thy showers from sky to sky.
Deepen the purple of the hills with thy
    majestic shadows, quicken the languid
    forests into flowers, and awaken in the
    hill-streams the fervour of the far-
    away quest.
Come to me like summer cloud, stirring
    my heart with the promise of hidden
    life, and the gladness of the green.

XXIX

I HAVE met thee where the night touches
the edge of the day; where the light
startles the darkness into dawn, and the
waves carry the kiss of the one shore to
the other.
From the heart of the fathomless blue
comes one golden call, and across the
dusk of tears I try to gaze at thy face and
know not for certain if thou art seen.

XXX

IF love be denied me then why does the
morning break its heart in songs, and
why are these whispers that the south
wind scatters among the new-born
leaves?
If love be denied me then why does the
midnight bear in yearning silence the
pain of the stars?
And why does this foolish heart recklessly
launch its hope on the sea whose end it
does not know?

XXXI

ONLY a portion of my gift is in this world,
the rest of it is in my dreams.

You, who ever elude my touch, come there
in secret silence, hiding your lamp.
I shall know you by the thrill in the dark-
ness, by the whisper of the unseen
worlds, by the breath of the unknown
shore—
I shall know you by the sudden delight of
my heart melting into sadness of tears.

XXXII

I KNOW you will win my heart some day,.
my lover.
Through your stars you gaze deep into
my dreams;
You send your secrets in your moonbeams
to me, and I muse and my eyes dim
with tears.
Your wooing is in the sunny sky thrilling
in the tremulous leaves, in the idle hours
overflowing with shepherds' piping, in
the rain-dimmed dusk when the heart
aches with its loneliness.

XXXIII

SOMEONE has secretly left in my hand
a flower of love.
Someone has stolen my heart and scat-
tered it abroad in the sky.

I know not if I have found him or I am
seeking him everywhere, if it is a pang
of bliss or of pain.

XXXIV

THE rains sweep the sky from end to end.
In the wild wet wind the jasmines revel
in their own perfume.
There is a secret joy in the bosom of the
night, it is the joy of the veiled sky in
its hidden stars, the joy of the midnight
forest in its hoarded bird-songs.
Let me fill my heart with it and carry it in
secret through the day.

XXXV

WHEN I travelled in the day I felt secure,
and I did not heed the wonder of thy
road, for I was proud of my speed; thy
own light stood between me and thy
presence.
Now it is night, and I feel thy road at
every step in the dark and the scent of
flowers filling the silence—like mother's
whisper to the child when the light is
out.
I hold tight thy hand and thy touch is
with me in my loneliness.

XXXVI

Sailing through the night I came to life's
feast, and the morning's golden goblet
was filled with light for me.

I sang in joy,

I knew not who was the giver,

And I forgot to ask his name.

In the midday the dust grew hot under
my feet and the sun overhead.

Overcome by thirst I reached the well.

Water was poured to me.

I drank it.

And while I loved the ruby cup that was
sweet as a kiss,

I did not see him who held it and forgot
to ask his name.

In the weary evening I seek my way
home.

My guide comes with a lamp and beckons
me.

I ask his name,

But I only see his light through the silence
and feel his smile filling the darkness.

XXXVII

Do not leave me and go, for it is night.

The road through the wilderness is lonely
and dark and lost in tangles:

The tired earth lies still, like one blind
and without a staff.
I seem to have waited for this moment for
ages to light my lamp and cull my
flowers.
I have reached the brink of the shoreless
sea to take my plunge and lose myself
forever.

XXXVIII

I DID not know that I had thy touch before
it was dawn.
The news has slowly reached me through
my sleep, and I open my eyes with its
surprise of tears.
The sky seems full of whispers for me and
my limbs are bathed with songs.
My heart bends in worship like a dew-
laden flower, and I feel the flood of my
life rushing to the endless.

XXXIX

No guest had come to my house for long,
my doors were locked, my windows bar-
red; I thought my night would be
lonely.
When I opened my eyes I found the dark-
ness had vanished.

I rose up and ran and saw the bolts of my
gates all broken, and through the open
door your wind and light waved their
banner.

When I was a prisoner in my own house,
and the doors were shut, my heart ever
planned to escape and to wander.

Now at my broken gate, I sit still and wait
for your coming,

You keep me bound by my freedom.

XL

PUT out the lamps, my heart, the lamps
of your lonely night.

The call comes to you to open your doors,
for the morning light is abroad.

Leave your lute in the corner, my heart,
the lute of your lonely life.

The call comes to you to come out in
silence, for the morning sings your own
songs.

XLI

THY gift of the earliest flower came to me
this morning, and came the faint tuning
of thy light.

I am a bee that has wallowed in the heart
of thy golden dawn,

My wings are radiant with its pollen.
I have found my place in the feast of songs
 in thy April, and I am freed of my
 fetters like the morning of its mist in a
 mere play.

XLII

FREE me as free are the birds of the wilds,
 the wanderers of unseen paths.
Free me as free are the deluge of rain, and
 as the storm that shakes its locks and
 rushes on to its unknown end.
Free me as free is the forest fire, as is the
 thunder that laughs aloud and hurls
 defiance to darkness.

XLIII

WHEN you called me I was asleep under
 the shadows of my walls and I did not
 hear you.
Then you struck me with your own hands
 and wakened me in tears.
I started up to see that the sun had risen,
 that the flood-tide had brought the
 call of the deep, and my boat was ready
 rocking on the dancing water.

XLIV

REJOICE!

For Night's fetters have broken, the
dreams have vanished.

Thy word has rent its veils, the buds of
morning are opened; awake, O sleeper!

Light's greetings spread from the East
to the West,

And at the ramparts of the ruined prison
rise the pæans of Victory!

XLV

IN this moment I see you seated upon
the morning's golden carpet.

The sun shines in your crown, the stars
drop at your feet, the crowds come and
bow to you and go, and the poet sits
speechless in the corner.

XLVI

MY guest has come to my door in this
autumn morning.

Sing, my heart, sing thy welcome!

Make thy song the song of the sunlit
blue, of the dew-damp air, of the lavish
gold of harvest fields, of the laughter of
the loud water.

Or stand mute before him for awhile
gazing at his face;
Then leave thy house and go out with him
in silence.

XLVII

I LIVED on the shady side of the road and
watched my neighbours' gardens across
the way revelling in the sunshine.
I felt I was poor, and from door to door
went with my hunger.
The more they gave me from their careless
abundance the more I became aware
of my beggar's bowl.
Till one morning. I awoke from my sleep
at the sudden opening of my door, and
you came and asked for alms.
In despair I broke the lid of my chest open
and was startled into finding my own
wealth.

XLVIII

THOU hast taken him to thine arms and
crowned him with death, him who ever
waited outside like a beggar at life's
feast.
Thou hast put thy right hand on his
failures and kissed him with peace that

stills life's turbulent thirst.
Thou hast made him one with all kings and with the ancient world of wisdom.

XLIX

In the world's dusty road I lost my heart, but you picked it up in your hand.
I gleaned sorrow while seeking for joy, but the sorrow which you sent to me has turned to joy in my life.
My desires were scattered in pieces, you gathered them and strung them in your love.
And while I wandered from door to door, every step led me to your gate.

L

I was with the crowd when I was in the road;
Where the road ends I find myself alone with you.
I knew not when my day dimmed into dusk and my companions left me.
I knew not when your doors opened and I stood surprised at my own heart's music.
But are there still traces of tears in my eyes

though the bed is made, the lamp is lit,
and we are alone, you and I?

LI

WHEN they came and clamoured and
surrounded me they hid thee from my
sight.
I thought I would bring to thee my gifts
last of all.
Now that the day has waned, and they
have taken their dues and left me alone,
I see thee standing at the door.
But I find I have no gift remaining to give,
and I hold both my hands up to thee.

LII

MUCH have you given to me,
Yet I ask for more—
I come to you not merely for the draught
of water, but for the spring;
Not for guidance to the door alone, but
to the Master's hall; not only for the
gift of love, but for the lover himself.

LIII

I HAVE come to thee to take thy touch
before I begin my day.

Let thy eyes rest upon my eyes for awhile.

Let me take to my work the assurance of thy comradeship, my friend.

Fill my mind with thy music to last through the desert of noise!

Let thy Love's sunshine kiss the peaks of my thoughts and linger in my life's valley where the harvest ripens.

LIV

Stand before my eyes, and let thy glance touch my songs into a flame.

Stand among thy stars and let me find kindled in their lights my own fire of worship.

The earth is waiting at the world's way-side;

Stand upon the green mantle she has flung upon thy path; and let me feel in her grass and meadow flowers the spread of my own salutation.

Stand in my lonely evening where my heart watches alone; fill her cup of solitude, and let me feel in me the infinity of thy love.

LV

LET thy love play upon my voice and rest on my silence.

Let it pass through my heart into all my movements.

Let thy love like stars shine in the darkness of my sleep and dawn in my awakening.

Let it burn in the flame of my desires.

And flow in all currents of my own love.

Let me carry thy love in my life as a harp does its music, and give it back to thee at last with my life.

LVI

You hide yourself in your own glory, my King.

The sand-grain and the dew-drop are more proudly apparent than yourself.

The world unabashed calls all things its own that are yours—yet it is never brought to shame.

You make room for us while standing aside in silence; therefore love lights her own lamp to seek you and comes to your worship unbidden.

LVII

When from the house of feast I came back
    home, the spell of the midnight quieted
    the dance in my blood.
My heart became silent at once like a
    deserted theatre with its lamps out.
My mind crossed the dark and stood
    among the stars, and I saw that we were
    playing unafraid in the silent courtyard
    of our King's palace.

LVIII

I was musing last night on my spendthrift
    days, when I thought you spoke to me—
' In youth's careless career you kept all
    the doors open in your house.
The world went in and out as it pleased—
    the world with its dust, doubts, and
    disorder—and with its music.
With the wild crowd I came to you again
    and again unknown and unbidden.
Had you kept shut your doors in wise
    seclusion how could I have found my
    way into your house?'

NONE needs be thrust aside to make room
    for you.
When love prepares your seat she prepares
    it for all.
Where the earthly King appears, guards
    keep out the crowd, but when you come,
    my King, the whole world comes in
    your wake.

WITH his morning songs he knocks at our
    door bringing his greetings of sunrise.
With him we take our cattle to the fields
    and play our flute in the shade.
We lose him to find him again and again
    in the market crowd.
In the busy hour of the day we come upon
    him of a sudden, sitting on the wayside
    grass.
We march when he beats his drum,
We dance when he sings.
We stake our joys and sorrows to play his
    game to the end.
He stands at the helm of our boat,
With him we rock on the perilous waves.
For him we light our lamp and wait when
    our day is done.

LXI

Run to his side as his comrades where he
  works with all workers.
Sit around him as his partners where he
  plays his games.
Follow him where he marches, keeping
  step to the rhythm of his drum-beats.
Rush into the thick of the fair—the fair
  of life and death—
For there he is with the crowd in the heart
  of its tumult.
Do not falter in your journey across the
  lonely hills over the thorns.
For his call sounds at every step and we
  know that it is love's voice.

LXII

When bells sounded in your temple in
  the morning, men and women hastened
  down the woodland path with their
  offerings of fresh flowers.
But I lay on the grass in the shade and
  let them pass by.
I think it was well that I was idle, for
  then my flowers were in bud.
At the end of the day they have bloomed,
  and I go to my evening worship.

LXIII

My King's road that lies still before my
house makes my heart wistful.
It stretches its beckoning hand towards
me; its silence calls me out of my home;
with dumb entreaties it kisses my feet
at every step.
It leads me on I know not to what
abandonment, to what sudden gain or
surprises of distress.
I know not where its windings end—
But my King's road that lies still before
my house makes my heart wistful.

LXIV

While I walk to my King's house at the
end of the day the travellers come to ask
me—
' What hast thou for King's tribute? '
I do not know what to show them or how
to answer, for I have merely this song.
My preparation is large in my house,
where the claim is much and many are
the claimants.
But when I come to my King's house I
have only this single song to offer it for
his wreath.

80

LXV

My songs are the same as are the spring
  flowers, they come from you.
Yet I bring these to you as my own.
You smile and accept them, and you are
  glad at my joy of pride.
If my song flowers are frail and they fade
  and drop in the dust, I shall never
  grieve.
For absence is not loss in your hand, and
  the fugitive moments that blossom in
  beauty are kept ever fresh in your
  wreath.

LXVI

My King, thou hast called me to play my
  flute at the roadside, that they who bear
  the burden of voiceless life may stop in
  their errands for a moment and sit
  and wonder before the balcony of thy
  palace gate; that they may see anew
  the ever old and find afresh what is ever
  about them, and say, 'The flowers are
  in bloom, and the birds sing.'

LXVII

When my first early songs woke in my

heart I thought they were the playmates of the morning flowers.

When they shook their wings and flew into the wilderness it seemed to me that they had the spirit of the summer which comes down with a sudden thunder roar to spend its all in laughter.

I thought that they had the mad call of the storm to rush and lose their way beyond the sunset land.

But now when in the evening light I see the blue line of the shore,

I know my songs are the boat that has brought me to the harbour across the wild sea.

LXVIII

THERE are numerous strings in your lute, let me add my own among them.

Then when you smite your chords my heart will break its silence and my life will be one with your song.

Amidst your numberless stars let me place my own little lamp.

In the dance of your festival of lights my heart will throb and my life will be one with your smile.

LXIX

LET my song be simple as the waking in
the morning, as the dripping of dew from
the leaves,
Simple as the colours in clouds and showers
of rain in the midnight.
But my lute strings are newly strung and
they dart their notes like spears sharp
in their newness.
Thus they miss the spirit of the wind and
hurt the light of the sky; and these
strains of my songs fight hard to push
back thy own music.

LXX

I HAVE seen thee play thy music in life's
dancing hall; in the sudden leaf-burst
of spring thy laughter has come to greet
me; and lying among field flowers I
have heard in the grass thy whisper.
The child has brought to my house the
message of thy hope, and the woman
the music of thy love.
Now I am waiting on the seashore to feel
thee in death, to find life's refrain back
again in the star songs of the night.

I REMEMBER my childhood when the sun-
rise, like my play-fellow, would burst
into my bedside with its daily surprise
of morning; when the faith in the mar-
vellous bloomed like fresh flowers in my
heart every day, looking into the face
of the world in simple gladness; when
insects, birds and beasts, the common
weeds, grass and the clouds had their
fullest value of wonder; when the patter
of rain at night brought dreams from
the fairyland, and mother's voice in the
evening gave meaning to the stars.

And then I think of death, and the rise
of the curtain and the new morning and
my life awakened in its fresh surprise of
love.

LXXII

WHEN my heart did not kiss thee in love,
O world, thy light missed its full
splendour and thy sky watched
through the long night with its lighted
lamp.

My heart came with her songs to thy side,
whispers were exchanged, and she put
her wreath on thy neck.

I know she has given thee something which will be treasured with thy stars.

LXXIII

Thou hast given me thy seat at thy window from the early hour.

I have spoken to thy silent servants of the road running on thy errands, and have sung with thy choir of the sky.

I have seen the sea in calm bearing its immeasurable silence, and in storm struggling to break open its own mystery of depth.

I have watched the earth in its prodigal feast of youth, and in its slow hours of brooding shadows.

Those who went to sow seeds have heard my greetings, and those who brought their harvest home or their empty baskets have passed by my songs.

Thus at last my day has ended and now in the evening I sing my last song to say that I have loved thy world.

LXXIV

It has fallen upon me, the service of thy singer.

In my songs I have voiced thy spring

flowers, and given rhythm to thy rustl-
ing leaves.

I have sung into the hush of thy night and
peace of thy morning.

The thrill of the first summer rains has
passed into my tunes, and the waving of
the autumn harvest.

Let not my song cease at last, my Master,
when thou breakest my heart to come
into my house, but let it burst into thy
welcome.

LXXV

GUESTS of my life,

You came in the early dawn, and you in
the night,

Your name was uttered by the Spring
flowers and yours by the showers of
rain.

You brought the harp into my house and
you brought the lamp.

After you had taken your leave I found
God's footprints on my floor.

Now when I am at the end of my pilgrim-
age I leave in the evening flowers of
worship my salutations to you all.

I FELT I saw your face, and I launched my
  boat in the dark.

Now the morning breaks in smiles and the
  spring flowers are in bloom.

Yet should the light fail and the flowers
  fade I will sail onward.

When you made mute signal to me the
  world slumbered and the darkness was
  bare.

Now the bells ring loud and the boat is
  laden with gold.

Yet should the bells become silent and
  my boat be empty I will sail onwrad.

Some boats have gone away and some are
  not ready, but I will not tarry
  behind.

The sails have filled, the birds come from
  the other shore.

Yet, if the sails droop, if the message of the
  shore be lost, I will sail onward.

LXXVII

' TRAVELLER, where do you go?'
' I go to bathe in the sea in the redd'ning
  dawn, along the tree-bordered path.'
' Traveller, where is that sea?'
' There where this river ends its course,

where the dawn opens into morning,
where the day droops to the dusk.

'Traveller, how many are they who
come with you?'

'I know not how to count them.

They are travelling all night with their
lamps lit, they are singing all day
through land and water.'

'Traveller, how far is the sea?'

'How far is it we all ask.

The rolling roar of its water swells to the
sky when we hush our talk.

It ever seems near yet far.'

'Traveller, the sun is waxing strong.

'Yes, our journey is long and grievous.

Sing who are weary in spirit, sing who are
timid of heart.'

'Traveller, what if the night overtakes
you?'

'We shall lie down to sleep till the new
morning dawns with its songs, and the
call of the sea floats in the air.'

LXXVIII

COMRADE of the road,
Here are my traveller's greetings to thee.
O Lord of my broken heart, of leave-
taking and loss, of the grey silence of the
dayfall,

My greetings of the ruined house to thee!
O Light of the new-born morning,
Sun of the everlasting day,
My greetings of the undying hope to thee!
My guide,
I am a wayfarer of an endless road,
My greetings of a wanderer to thee.

Crossing

Index of First Words

91

MACMILLAN POCKET TAGORE